In His Time

In His Time

A Story of Grief, Hope and Faith

ANGELA ARMSTRONG

In His Time
Published by Angela Armstrong
with Castle Publishing Ltd
New Zealand

© 2022 Angela Armstrong

ISBN 978-0-473-62376-0 (Softcover)
ISBN 978-0-473-62377-7 (ePUB)
ISBN 978-0-473-62378-4 (Kindle)

Editing:
Sally Webster

Production & Typesetting:
Andrew Killick
Castle Publishing Services
www.castlepublishing.co.nz

Cover Design:
Paul Smith

All Scripture quotations, unless otherwise indicated,
are taken from the Holy Bible, New International Version®, NIV®.
Copyright ©1973, 1978, 1984, 2011 by Biblica, Inc.™
Used by permission of Zondervan.
All rights reserved worldwide.

ALL RIGHTS RESERVED

No part of this publication may be reproduced,
stored in a retrieval system, or transmitted
in any form or by any means, electronic, mechanical,
photocopying, recording or otherwise,
without prior written permission from the author.

Dedicated to My Four Precious Children

You are all amazing. I couldn't be prouder of the adults you've become.

The thing each and every one of us needs in life, especially when going through adversity, is to *breathe* – just *breathe*.

At first, it's minute by minute, then hour by hour... then the months start rolling by, and you just have to remember to do the basics. Nothing else is required. Take walks, get out in nature – it's an antidepressant, it's God-given and it's free to all.

Surround yourself with good people and enjoy them – they can be a great anchor of positive words and encouragement.

Always be kind to each other, watch your words.

Above all, *pray* – put your trust and hope in the Lord.

Remember, in life there will always be change. (Like a caterpillar becoming a beautiful butterfly.)

You are never the same person after going through adversity, but you can and will come out of it stronger. Let God in and trust Him. He never promised we wouldn't go through tough times, but he does promise to be with us as we walk the journey.

Love you all,
Mum xxxx

Contents

Acknowledgements	9
In His Time	11
Why Gary?	15
No Words	19
Grief-Stricken	21
Recollections	23
Shattered Dreams	29
Meeting God, and Gary	31
Gary's Notes	33
New Beginnings	37
Looking Back	41
11 January 1989	43
The Next Day...	45
And All the Days After That...	47
Choosing to Live with Purpose	51
Moving On	53
Looking Up	59
Memories	61
The Funeral Home	63
The Funeral	65
The Aftermath	67
Marriage	69
The Supernatural	71
The Father's Heart	75
Time with the Lord	77

Walking Through the Valley	81
Insensitivity	83
Random Thoughts	85
Coping with Grief	87
Anxiety	91
Acres of Hope	93
Disillusioned	99
Church Life	101
God's Promises	103
From Despair to Faith	105
A Relationship with God	109
In Closing	111
The Beginning?	113

Acknowledgements

THANKS TO Stacey, Tania, Jude and Chantelle from Soul Church Matamata for your encouragement and for being there to support me. You are true sisters in Christ.

To my beautiful sisters and best friends, Leanne and Karen – thank you for your constant support in helping me through my life journey; I love you both very much.

Thanks to Mum for always being there to support me, and for your constant prayers.

Thanks to the Lord for Your ongoing patience, and for continually extending Your hand to me. Thank you, Lord, for being there regardless of where I am. You are my truly amazing and magnificent Friend. Thank you for leading all my roads back to you, for I know I always can trust You.

To my children, Larissa, Rebecca, Luke and Eden – I love each of you very much; you are the most precious people I could ever have wished to bring into this world. I am so proud of the closeness we share as a family. I am extremely proud of the love you have for each other. I am proud of the beautiful partners you have all chosen to do life with; they are an amazing addition to our family.

Vaughan, thank you for being so good and kind. For holding my hand and choosing to walk with me through this season. Thank you for helping me raise our four beautiful children. You are amazing. In our journey together you have been strong and faithful. You are a man of true character, a truly precious gift, and I thank God for you.

In His Time

THIS IS A STORY OF GRIEF, loss and hope. My prayer in writing it is that people all over the world will be blessed by what they read. There is so much pain in the world as a result of difficulties and tragedies of many and various kinds. I pray that those reading this book will gain further understanding and deeper empathy for those travelling that hard road of suffering. I pray that those currently on that road will realise that this hard time they are going through will not go on for the rest of their lives. That pain need not stay with them forever, and they can choose not to allow it to consume them – in this way, over time, they will find a path back to leading a fully-functional life again.

I also pray that all of us in our various trials will realise that we can choose to have a relationship with the Lord Jesus Christ, and that He will restore us. That is not to say that our problems will go away immediately – but that God can take what has harmed us and turn it into something that will work out as a blessing in our lives. He has the power to do the seemingly impossible.

For those of you who have *not* lost a loved one, I hope this book gives you insight into the depth of sorrow some people have to face. I hope it will help you understand the horrors of grief others have gone through after losing a loved one. And that you will develop greater awareness of and deeper empathy for what they are going through.

One of the themes of this book is the battle I had between grief, hurt and God. God always wanted to be there for me (and was), but He seemed distant because I was feeling hurt, disappointed and let down. Losing my husband was not the plan I had for my life, and I knew God could have changed the circumstances and the outcome of that day. So grief took me on a journey of coming to terms with that, and getting my head around the fact that God's ways are not always our ways. As time went by, I discovered His presence in the pain.

I am definitely not the most qualified person to be writing a book. I never dreamt I would actually do so. But when the Lord placed it on my heart, I felt such an urgency that I did not stop to question my ability. It took me a long time to move past all the questions in my mind. But eventually I was ready to be obedient to what my Lord had asked me to do, and I embarked on this journey with Him.

Living a purpose-filled life is a privilege, and it has turned my heartbreak valley into acres of hope.

Faith is the key. If you have faith, the Lord will 'open the sea' for you. All you need to do is to step out in faith, and He will do the rest. Make sure that you grow a life of victory, rather than one of fear.

Recently, whilst out spraying weeds on the farm, I was in deep thought about a book I was reading at the time. This triggered a thought that had every now and then over the past ten years popped into my head – the idea of writing a book about the events that had taken place in my life. Although I had mentioned the idea to a few people, it always ended up being relegated into the 'too-hard' or 'don't-want-to-go-there' baskets. However this time something was different, and the Lord really convicted me that I needed to take it seriously. I now felt both excited and emotional at the same time. So I said to the Lord, 'If you want me to do this, I need to be really convinced; I need confirmation.' I needed to know without a doubt this was from Him and not just my imagination. A short time later I arrived home, only to receive a text from my friend asking me to meet her for coffee. When I got to her house I told her about my talk with the Lord, and how I thought He wanted me to tell my story. She then said that just a few weeks prior to this she had met a lady who held weekend retreats for aspiring writers. This was my first confirmation.

Attending Soul Church that night, I listened as one of the pastors talked about stepping out in faith, and wondered if that was another confirmation. And so they kept on coming, on and on – so much so that I have lost count of them all.

The day I was out in the paddock and talking with the Lord about writing this book, I got a picture in my head of the Israelites just as they were about to step into the Red Sea (see Exodus 14:14-22). I noted their obedience as they followed the Lord's instructions, and how as they did so the waters parted for them. What an amazing picture of obedience. They would no doubt have been wondering if in fact those waters actually *were* going to part just as the Lord had told Moses they would. What courage it must have taken for them to take those first steps! I needed to find that same faith to strengthen me, so that I could write about my journey through grief.

You will notice that the story of my loss moves backwards and forwards through time, revisiting certain situations, and forming a kind of collage of the events that unfolded in my life and the things I've learnt along the way. Grief is like that – it's doesn't follow a simple timeline from start to finish. There are good days, and not so good days – days when you look to the future and other days when memories of the past come flooding back.

But through it all, God is gracious – leading, teaching, comforting and restoring. I've found that to be true in my journey, and I know He wants it to be true in yours too.

At times on this journey the valleys get very dark, but we need

In His Time

to remember that the sun will rise tomorrow. In time, with His help, we will learn to clothe ourselves with a newfound purpose and strength that would make our loved one proud.

May God bless you all!
Angela

Why Gary?

I REALISE NOW THAT I will only know the answer to this question when I get to Heaven. But, the older I get and the more I read about Heaven in the Bible, I think that will be the last thing on my mind when I get there. I am sure that at that time, because we will be so caught up in the joy of being reunited with those loved ones we haven't seen in a while, nothing else will matter.

Paul tells us in 2 Corinthians 5:8 that, for Christians, to be absent from the body means to be present with the Lord. That begs the question – can you 'lose' someone if you know exactly where they are?

At the end of this earthly life, whether we are going to Heaven or Hell, the afterlife will be more real than the one we are living now. In a flash, Gary left this world and was immediately with His Lord, and no doubt full of joy. And it is that reassurance that has got me through my pain. That absolute knowing without a doubt that Gary is in Heaven with the Lord has been my saving grace.

I was never offered any form of therapy, so I am hoping that in writing this book I will find complete healing. I am trusting the Lord to do this for me.

Over the weeks and months after Gary's funeral I got stared at whenever I went to town. I remember seeing people talking and pointing at me, and then quickly crossing the road so they didn't have to talk to or acknowledge me. I most often would be walking with my mum, and I remember talking about it with her as we saw it happening.

How real it all felt in that time – that all-consuming pain in my heart, as if it were being ripped out. And that awful feeling stayed with me for a long, long time. I remember trying to act normal and to push myself to keep going, when inside I felt desperate, lost and so alone.

The physical pain in my heart! The horror of feeling that Gary had been ripped out of it. I remember thinking, 'So it's true – you *can* actually have a broken heart.' The lyrics of the Country love songs I had grown up listening to, all those sad words about broken hearts, suddenly felt so real.

Up to that time I hadn't thought that resilience was one of my strong points, but now that I look back I can see that my lowest moments were actually the times when I was at my strongest, in so many ways.

There's a well-known old story about a person walking with God along a beach – a symbol of life's journey. Looking back and seeing only one set of footprints in the sand, the person asks why God had left her alone in those difficult times. And God replies, 'My precious child, I love you and will never leave you. Never, ever, during your trials and testings. When you saw only one set of footprints, it was then that I carried you.' I was in a 'Footprints in the Sand' situation – where the Lord was carrying me.

Somehow, the Lord and I had become a team. I really don't know where I would be now if I hadn't had my Lord and trusty Friend with me. At times I became lost and lived in my own strength, seeking out the things of this world. In fact I spent years trying to manage things in my own strength; but it never worked out well, and I always wandered back to Him. And He alone has been my strength through it all.

I now can actually thank the Lord for what I have been through, because I am able to fully appreciate the unbearable pain that other people also go through. I am also incredibly thankful for the three-and-a-half years I had of knowing Gary, and the incredible eight months of being married. My greatest blessings are the time I had with Gary and the new life I have today.

Recently, whilst writing this book, I looked back over photos of my last moments with Gary. I reflected on the faces in the photo. Everyone looked solemn; but as I looked at myself tucking him in the coffin, all that could be seen on my face was pure love. I can remember sobbing so hard just a few minutes after that, as I was leaving. It didn't feel right to have to leave him there. Everyone was unbearably upset, and even the undertaker looking after Gary had tears running down his face. When I thought about it later, it meant so much to me that even he'd had so much compassion.

I remember the first time my parents drove me over to Hamilton to visit Gary at the funeral home, with several other family members following behind us. I was feeling both nervous and excited. I was excited about seeing him and holding his hand again. I had missed him so much. It had been three days since the accident, when I had last seen him. That felt like such a long time, for up to then I had seen him every day since we had met.

Sitting in the back seat of the car, I remember singing that old redemption song, 'Father, I place into Your hands the way that I should go, for I know I always can trust You.' Reflecting back on it now, I wonder what my parents would have been thinking at the time. Afterwards I can remember wondering where it had come from and why I had sung it in that moment. We sang it in church sometimes, but it was not a song that usually came to mind. Throughout the years I have often marvelled that it was placed on my heart. The words of that song were so incredibly perfect for that time, and they have been very special to me ever since then. I think the Lord must have been stilling my heart, as I felt such peace at that moment. I just wanted to see Gary and spend time with him. I missed him so very much.

Later on down the track, my Heavenly Father was still there with me all the time, in many different ways. Sometimes He was there to engulf me – like during the first few days – and seeing to all my needs. At other times He just turned up in a song that would quiet my heart, and at others He put his arms around me and I felt so protected. At the funeral I remember having an overwhelming impression that Gary was with me, that he was sitting so close. At times I was lost in the moment, but when I think back I realise that the Holy Spirit was so protective, so close, that there are no words to describe it. By earthly reckoning, there was no way of getting through a tragedy like that at 22 years of age the way I did. My only coping tool was my faith in the Lord and the support of my family and friends.

Also, Gary's older brother and his wife were absolutely wonderful to me, and the most amazing support. Most weekends for the next 20 months after the accident they opened their home and family to me. Most Friday afternoons I would get in my car and travel out to stay with them. It was amazing to be able to just sit and chat. They were both absolutely incredible. Wendy would sit up and talk with me into the early hours of the morning; hour upon hour she sat patiently listening to me pouring my heart out to her. I realise now how incredibly selfless she was, to continually be there for me in such a big way. I desperately needed them, and they were there for me completely. I love them both very much and am grateful I have had them in my life for the entire journey. I was and always will be very appreciative.

No Words

I KNOW WHAT I EXPERIENCED at the time of losing Gary, but it is very hard to try to explain those feelings. I remember being filled with the Holy Spirit, and how He took control and filled my mind so that I felt at peace a lot of the time. I'm not sure if 'control' is the right word, but I will just try to explain the best I can. Rather than being an outer-body experience, it was more of an all-consuming sense of being gently led. It was subtle, comforting and kind. It was as if a gentle awareness or Presence was consuming me.

I remember thinking that people would soon be arriving, even though I didn't yet know what exactly had happened, I did know that Gary had gone missing. I was told to ring someone, so I remember ringing my mother and saying, 'Gary has gone missing down at the waterhole.' That is all I had been told, and all I knew for the next couple of hours. I locked the dog up and had a quick shower because I had milked that afternoon. A friend rung me on the phone – we had planned to go out that evening – and I remember telling her that Gary had gone missing. She then phoned some people from our church to come and help look for him.

God's peace consumed my body and mind, and I now realise that in those moments I was experiencing His ultimate gift, His precious Holy Spirit. And He has been with me ever since. At the time I didn't know it was the Holy Spirit I was experiencing, I guess because I had never experienced Him like that before. The Lord was now my protector. He knew what had taken place down at the river that evening and was preparing everything around me for what lay ahead.

During the first few days after the accident I would sit and think about Gary; he consumed every thought, even wishing I could embalm his body and place it in the corner of my living room. Just to be able to look at him once again and hold his hand would have been amazing. Someone who hasn't lived through the death of a partner or loved one would probably think that sounds so crazy, but I was so desperate to keep him near me in any way possible. In such a situation your thoughts get so desperate that you wish for things that seem bizarre; you would do anything to keep your loved one with you.

I prayed: 'God, you made me to have joy, but this seems so far away right now.'

Grief-Stricken

I HAD BEEN LOOKING FORWARD to spending the rest of my life with Gary. Now, in a moment, he was gone. It's a strange thing, to have all your plans in place thinking life will go on per usual – and all of a sudden to be left with nothing but thoughts and memories. It's very hard for a young 22-year-old girl to process all that. It took a very long time to do so, but thankfully not an entire lifetime.

When I met him, Gary was a car painter and was just finishing his studies. He had always dreamt about trying his hand at farming, and on 1 June – about two weeks after our wedding – he started his new farm job. He really loved farming and took to it like a duck to water. In December he signed up for a much larger job milking cows; he was in a hurry to get ahead and had so many plans.

> *The Lord is close to the broken-hearted and saves those who are crushed in spirit.* (Psalm 34:18)

Recollections

Whoever dwells in the shelter of the Most High, will rest in the shadow of the Almighty. I will say of the Lord, 'He is my refuge and my fortress, my God in whom I trust.' (Psalm 91:1-2)

I DON'T KNOW IF I WOULD have made it through if I hadn't been told about what had happened to Mum after I had called her to say Gary had gone missing. Here she tells it in her own words:

It was a lovely summer's day on the 11th of January 1989. Angela's father Dave and I were at home when at approximately 6.25 pm we got a phone-call from her to say that Gary had been swimming in the river with two others and had gone missing. In that moment, whilst still on the phone, I experienced a very clear vision of Gary. He suddenly appeared, just his face, and it shone. He said, 'Hi Mum (he always called me Mum, right from the first day we met), I am OK. I'm happy and don't worry.' Then he disappeared. Immediately I knew Gary had died and that he was with his Lord and Saviour.

I called out to Dave, who was working out in the shed, and told him what had happened. He dropped everything and immediately left for the river to search for Gary. I rang the police and told them what had happened, and they said they would pick me up and take me to the river with them. While I was waiting for them to arrive, I rang my three other children to let them know what I knew. The police arrived and we travelled very fast, not wasting any time. There were already friends and relatives gathered there by the time we arrived. Dave was walking along the riverbank calling out to Gary, but there was no answer.

Our daughter's world was now completely turned upside down. They had only been married for eight months, and we were all in deep shock and disbelief. What a terrible thing to happen. We were not sure if we were dreaming. Filled with feelings of deep sadness, we had moments of panic come over us. Our emotions were all over the place, and there were lots of tears.

Do you ever get over a thing like this? I don't think so. It has such an impact on your life that you never forget it. We all deal with grief in different ways, and we have had to learn to live with it. But the one thing I am sure of is this – Gary is now with his Lord and Saviour.

The only person on earth I would believe with a story like that is Mum, because up until that moment she had always been very conservative in her thinking, and that was why her vision was so believable to me. Because of it, I am confident and secure in the knowledge of God's greatness. After hearing this, we immediately knew that Gary was experiencing Heaven at that very moment. What a wonderful gift of assurance God had given us.

Earlier that day, before the accident, I can remember spending the morning chipping thistles with Gary; or, rather, I was sitting on the bike talking to him while he did the work! The people we were employed by had a large decorated Christmas tree at the front of their house. It was huge, and covered in lights. Gary and I had taken all the lights down; it must have taken us a good hour or two to do so. After that I had been scheduled to do milking in the second cowshed; so at about three o'clock Gary dropped me down there. I remember saying, 'See you later; I love you.' That was the last thing I said to him before he headed back to the main cowshed.

Prior to this, Gary had said that he was planning to head out to the river sometime, in order to check out the swimming hole, and asked if I would like to go with him. I declined, telling him I would head home after milking to get dinner ready. I remember watching them from the kitchen window as they headed off into the distance. Gary had a couple of farm workers with him, as well as his 8-year-old nephew, who was staying with us for a week of the Christmas holidays.

It was an extremely hot January day, so they were all looking forward to getting into the river to cool off after the night's milking. When they arrived they kicked their gumboots off at the water's edge and got straight in. They were just beside a bridge and a rest area on State Highway 27. Our boss had told Gary about a nice waterhole a bit further downstream, and he had been wanting to check it out for a while. The older guy finished swimming and headed home, and Gary asked his nephew if he would like to go down river with him, offering to carry him on his back. The 17-year-old farm worker decided to go with them.

The three of them set off for the waterhole, Gary bouncing along with his nephew on his back. At this stage the river became very narrow and had blackberry bushes growing on both banks. The farm worker, who was just ahead of Gary, arrived at the waterhole first. Gary's feet had been able to touch the bottom most of the way there but, little did he know, the waterhole was ten meters deep. To make matters worse, the water level was up that day as there had been heavy rains a few days earlier.

With the weight of his nephew on his back, Gary arrived at the waterhole. As soon as he stepped into it, he sank beneath the surface, taking water into his lungs. Surfacing very briefly, he managed to push his nephew towards the bank, which was just one metre away. Even though it was so close, Gary couldn't reach it himself – all he could manage was to cry out a muffled 'help', and then he sank. It had taken all of his strength to push his nephew towards that riverbank, where he knew he would be safe.

Gary was 6-foot 2-inches tall and had been physically fit. The police later told us that in these situations, when water hits your lungs it immediately saps your energy and basically paralyses you. The young worker who was ahead of them heard his soft cry for help, but when he turned around Gary was nowhere to be seen, and he was unsure exactly where he had gone under. Panicking, he left the little boy alone on the bank of the waterhole and raced home to get help. Thankfully the child was okay. I'm not sure who came to that little boy's rescue or how he got back home, but I am extremely thankful that he too didn't drown.

Meanwhile the younger farm worker arrived breathlessly at our glass sliding door and said, 'Gary's gone missing; ring someone!' That's all he told me, and so I rang Mum. I think the guy must have been in so much shock that he just didn't have the words to explain more. As a result, I had absolutely no knowledge of what had happened, nor was I told until a couple of hours later.

After I rang Mum, she rang my sisters and our brother. Karen stayed at the house in order to contact people to help us. Leanne and I went quickly down to the river. We ran around in the long grass yelling things like, 'Gary, come out! Stop being silly! This is no longer a joke!'

I was feeling extremely panicky, and kept collapsing. I must have been in shock. I remember feeling very annoyed that he was not coming out of hiding. At that point I had no idea that anything really bad had happened. Gary was such a joker that I thought he was just being silly.

But eventually panic started to set in, and I was getting weaker; so we decided to head back home. Once we got back home, I remember more and more people arriving, and the pain in my chest growing significantly. I began experiencing feelings I had never felt before. Numbness. Panic. And nobody could tell me what had happened to Gary. *Wednesday 11 January 1989.* There was no way I could have ever imagined, not even in my wildest of dreams, that this would be the last day I would see him alive.

Shattered Dreams

WHEN SOMEBODY YOU LOVE DIES, you miss their touch, their smell, their voice and their very presence. You long to go back to the way things used to be. Your mind dwells on all the might-have-beens. At the time I felt fragile; I would smile, but it was just the movement of my mouth and nothing else. I was careful with my words; I tried not to ever show the true extent of my suffering and how vulnerable I was feeling. I let only a few people see me in that really fragile state. I kept those moments as much as I could to myself. It all got released when I was by myself in my car or my bedroom.

Over the years that followed I simply eased my pain with smoking and, at times, drinking alcohol. This gave me temporary relief; it relaxed me and allowed me to escape my loneliness.

Then there was all the legal stuff that needed sorting out. The signing of the papers from the bank and the lawyer, all with 'deceased' stamped on them. This made it seem so final, and I didn't want it to be. You are there signing it because you have to, but in your head you're thinking what a nightmare the whole process is. I longed to reach out to someone that could understand, someone else my age who had gone through something similar. But there was no one. Back then there was no social media, so it was not easy to link up with others.

Meeting God, and Gary

I BECAME A CHRISTIAN at an Easter camp at Tōtara Springs in Matamata when I was eight or nine years old. I remember the marquee; it was huge and crammed full of people. At the end of the service the speaker asked if anyone wanted to come up to the front and ask the Lord into their life. Gosh, I now realise how brave I was to do that in front of so many people. And how that *one* decision has shaped my life!

I have definitely tried doing things in my own strength a lot of the time since then, and this saw me walking away from God to chase what I perceived would be a good time, doing many things I shouldn't have been doing. I definitely always loved the Lord; I just thought I knew better a lot of the time.

Ten years after that, when I was about 18 years old, I met Gary. He had never been to a church service before, so I offered to take him the next Sunday night, if he wanted to. Walking in, he was very nervous, and chose to sit at the very end of the row of seats so that he could leave if he wanted to. But he ended up staying for the whole service and loved it. It wasn't long before he asked the Lord into his heart and started to read his Bible. He studied and studied that Bible. He asked so many questions of my dad and many other people at our church. He truly took his new-found faith very seriously.

At his funeral I remember one of the older men and one of his friends talking about that particular aspect of his life, and expressing the fact that the Lord himself can now answer all his questions.

Because many of the questions Gary asked were so deep, sometimes even the Elders struggled to answer them.

Gary was a 'full on' guy. If he was into something – anything – he was in there boots and all. He was a larger-than-life character that everyone was drawn to and loved. He very quickly became part of the church and talked about it constantly. He joined a Bible study group, and when we got engaged he moved in with a couple from the church. He absolutely adored that couple. Gary also started playing the drums in the church band; he loved it and enjoyed being part of the music group.

We got married on 14 May 1988. It was a beautiful wedding day, and we had lots of fun. Gary was always very happy and positive, and simply the most beautiful person to hang out with. I felt so blessed that this special person loved and adored me. At times he had to drag me to church because I didn't have his same enthusiasm. I suppose that's because I had been brought up going to church with my parents every Sunday, both morning and evening services, and I very much took it for granted.

Gary's Notes

WHEN GARY BECAME A CHRISTIAN and asked the Lord into his heart, he had a sense of urgency. He was in a rush to know all he could. The following are the church notes that I found in a drawer after he died. These are Gary's own 'super-gorgeous' words:

True worship: To worship the Lord God and to do so in the beauty of holiness.

The only true and acceptable form of worship is with a 'Whole Heart'.

Sinners still in sin cannot worship the Lord.

Do we worship for what we have done for Him, or for what He has done for us?

It is easy to worship the Lord!!

Just look outside at the wonders God has created. He has done so much for us.

When we have God on our side we have warmth, caring, loving and above all we have someone who is with us 24 hours a day.

How many of us ring a friend at 2.00 am in the morning because you want to talk about something? How many of us can say our friend won't tell anyone?

When we are scared God will comfort us and say, 'it's all right, I am with you'.

God can do all of this!

All we have to do is say, 'God, I know I am a sinner; I need you to help me and come into my life; I thank you for letting your son die for me and I thank you for making me new.' If we do this, God will give us the gift we all should have – ETERNAL LIFE.

This also means that we will have a few problems doing this because, man, it won't be easy; man, I enjoy doing the things I do that are wrong. So does Satan; he loves you doing them too. Because it means he can drag you down with him.

God says, 'come to me and I will protect you and forgive you, if you mean you are sorry.' You may think that if you become a Christian that your friends will laugh at you and tease you. Well, if that is so, they must not have been good friends to start off with. Just saying that if people think Christians are weird, to be honest I think they were probably weird before they ever became Christians.

The Lord loves us and wants us in His kingdom with Him. All you have to do is choose. God has a plan for everyone.

I loved Gary's character. He was always happy in the Lord. He had a warm, larger than life character, he was outgoing; he could lift the atmosphere in a room, just by walking into it. He always had purpose in his heart. He had a mind made-up, and never wavered in his convictions. Also, he was open and honest, and he had a real and rich relationship with Jesus Christ.

The following Bible verse was on a calendar in our house the day Gary died, so would have been the last verse he ever read:

> I am with you and will protect you wherever you go and will bring you back safely to this land. I will be with you constantly, until I have given you all I have promised. (Genesis 28:15, version unknown)

What an interesting and appropriate verse. Only God could have matched that verse for that day.

Gary's Notes

The following verse (the gospel in a nutshell) was his favourite and is featured on his headstone. This was the verse Gary lived by:

For God so loved the world that he gave his one and only Son, that whoever believes in him shall not perish but have eternal life. (John 3:16)

And this is a verse that completely sums up Gary's heart:

As water reflects the face, one's life reflects the heart. (Proverbs 27:19)

New Beginnings

EVEN AFTER GARY'S DEATH and all the amazing experiences surrounding it, I was still a hard nut to crack. I still very much enjoyed going to parties, drinking and smoking. I loved the feeling of being defiant, at times doing things that were definitely not pleasing to my God. This only served to show me His ongoing grace and patience with me. I would show up at church and really enjoy it, but my heart wasn't fully connected, by any stretch of the imagination. I was still too much enamoured with worldly things to fully surrender my life to Him.

This pattern of life lasted until my early fifties. By then I had a new and very supportive husband, and four beautiful adult children. Only then did I finally come back to the Lord and fully surrender my life to Him. I now wanted to live to love and honour Him.

In writing this book I want to honour Gary and his deep and beautiful faith in the Lord. But even more I want to honour the Lord for his steadfast love – that was and is always there. It never left me, even in my lowest times. I am so thankful to Him that as a little girl I had faith and was brave enough to ask Him into my heart. That *one* decision shaped the rest of my life more than anything else has. Now I am happy and content in my relationship with God. He was truly there through my darkest times, preparing me for what was to come. And to this day He has never let me down.

Despite this I still had many questions that remain yet unanswered: Why did all this happen in the first place? And why Gary?

Why did I have to go through all of this? Why was I given the special privilege of experiencing God so strongly? Do all Christians experience this type of thing? Why is the spiritual side of what I felt far clearer in my memory than all the human stuff?

I still don't know why I had the very sad but unique privilege of going through all of this. For years I never really talked about the spiritual things that happened because I felt they were so personal, and I didn't want people judging or questioning me regarding them. They were such beautiful moments that I just wanted to hold them dear to me. Since then, however, God has convicted me to share my testimony, in the belief that He will use it as a means of encouragement to many other people.

What I *do* know is that I went through a massive ordeal and that I experienced God right there in the midst of it all. I also know, without a doubt, that I could not have survived that pain if it hadn't been for the Lord carrying me and keeping me close to Him.

To be honest, there were moments when I wished it could be all over. Like the times when I was out in the car on my own and the thought of pulling over in front of an oncoming truck crossed my mind. I just wanted to escape the sheer pain of it all, to escape my new reality. I became derailed at times. But I always knew in the back of my mind that doing something like that would not make Gary proud of me; so I would just focus on getting through the day. Each time I had these dark thoughts, the Lord would counteract them with a pleasant memory from my childhood. In those moments, when I felt it was all too much, the Lord always reminded me that my life wasn't mine to take and that it belonged to Him.

But the questions kept on coming: What did God want me to learn by going through this experience? Was it to better understand the pain others carry? Was it to show me what it felt like to have a close relationship with Him?

New Beginnings

I do know I got through it all because of prayer. My mum and dad, as well as many other members of my church, all have very strong faith – and I know all of their prayers would have been powerful.

My life was turned upside down and inside out but, thanks to God hearing and answering my prayers, I managed to survive.

It took many years before I realised that God had a purpose for my going through all that I did. I am sure that nothing we go through in life is wasted, if we let God use it. He is the great Miracle Worker, who restores us and remoulds our lives. We simply have to be willing to choose Him and then listen to Him – and not be distracted by all the other things in life that compete for our attention.

> *And we know that in all things God works for the good of those who love him, who have been called according to his purpose.* (Romans 8:28)

> *But those who hope in the Lord will renew their strength, they will sour on wings like eagles, they will run and not grow weary, they will walk and not be faint.* (Isaiah 40:31)

> *So with you: Now is your time of grief, but I will see you again and you will rejoice, and no one will take away your joy.* (John 16:22)

Looking Back

LOOKING BACK, THERE IS SOMETHING I wish I had done after Gary died. I regret not having thought about writing down the many things I remember about our life together: our conversations, the things we loved, our plans (both big and small), our outings, and the things we loved to do together.

I do remember our holidays with all my family; they are such amazingly happy memories. Gary loved to go fishing with my dad. I remember that after Mum and Dad sold their share in the family bach they bought a caravan. We would all regularly go to a campsite at Whitianga. I remember one holiday when Karen and Kevin (my eldest sister and her husband), who were newly-weds at the time, were there with us all. My younger sister and I were sleeping in the caravan with Mum and Dad; the guys were sleeping on stretchers in the awning. I remember that night hearing a lot of laughter outside, only to find that Gary had flicked my younger sister's boyfriend's stretcher up on its end, sending him flying out the side of the awning. By this time we were all out there having a good laugh. There were heaps more amusing times like that; Gary was always the one to get up to funny business.

As time goes by, it gets harder and harder to remember specific incidents like that. Looking back, I now realise that I spent a lot of energy trying to hold on to all of those memories. I did this for the first two years or so after his death. Then life started filling up with other things that distracted me and, as time went by, some of those memories have faded. No matter how desperately I tried holding on to them all, one by one they started fading as I became more and more occupied with the new things in my life. I think it's a great thing that life at that stage started changing, but I still wish I had written down the memories of our life together.

Even though time passed and life started filling up with other things again, I always tried to keep the memory of Gary close. Even after I remarried and had children, he was always still a big part of our family. Growing up, my kids knew about 'Uncle Gary'. I often talked to them about him, so it felt like he was somehow still part of our family. When I think back on it now, I realise this was because I was still not wanting to let go of him. As long as he was part of our conversations, I felt he was still there in some way.

11 January 1989

On the night Gary went missing, just as it was getting dark, the Morrinsville Police came back to the house and asked if they could speak to me on my own in the bedroom. I remember them telling me that Gary was presumed drowned, and that they could not locate his body. They said they had put down nets so that if he was in the waterhole, then he would not be swept downstream by the movements of the water. They also told me that the diving squad from Wellington would be coming up the next day to locate his body. I remember telling them that he was all right as I knew that Gary was in Heaven and was happy. The finality of it all hadn't sunk in yet. I had seen him only a few hours before that, and the whole thing seemed surreal.

I remember asking the man who had married us to please stay on watch at the river overnight, just in case Gary crawled out of the river and needed help. Much later on he told me that sitting there at the waterhole had been the eeriest night he could remember. But he did it, nonetheless, and it meant the world to me. I was still clinging to the hope that Gary was alive, and that the police and everyone else had got it all wrong.

I stayed that night in town with my parents. In fact, I ended up staying there for just under two years. I am forever grateful that my family was living nearby and that I could just move back into their home and benefit from their love and support. I think that if Gary and I had moved away after we got married, then things might have been harder in that respect.

I can still remember how I felt heading back to Mum and Dad's place; like I was engulfed in a cloud of exhaustion. I was still holding on hard to the hope that it was all a mistake, a bad dream.

That first night felt very eerie. I remember everyone trying to get some sleep but ending up walking about the house.

The Next Day...

AT ABOUT 5.00 AM THE NEXT MORNING there was a knock at the door. It was a guy who lived two doors down. He had arrived with his dinghy on the back of his car and wanted Dad to go with him to look for Gary. Over that time everyone was incredibly kind; it was just amazing that people you didn't even expect it from would do such thoughtful things.

In every way, God was working behind the scenes the whole time. Just the simple fact that I hadn't gone swimming with them that day was a mercy; I definitely know I couldn't have handled being there. I think I would probably have drowned looking for him.

When I look back, I realise that the Holy Spirit was preparing us, as He knew how that day was going to play out. I can now look back and see the Lord's fingerprints all over that whole day and the days that followed.

At lunchtime, the police diving squad arrived at the waterhole. One of them was a Christian, so they all prayed with him before entering the water.

I was not allowed to be there, and had to stay at home. But being surrounded by like-minded people, I felt at peace, and was thankful to God for showing me that He had everything under control. It felt so comforting to me in that time, knowing that God had placed just the right person there. I had never met him before, and it was just his job, but that didn't matter. I felt so blessed that in the midst of everything that was happening around me, I could still feel and recognise that it was a God-moment. The Lord was clearly with me, and I realised it even at that dreadful time.

I remember sometime later the phone ringing; it was Dad to say that Gary's body had been found. I was utterly devastated.

Much later I remember feeling grateful that a Christian diver had been there to help pull him out. Only God could have orchestrated that. It was such a special blessing. I was told Gary had looked peaceful and beautiful. Flowers, cards and visitors started pouring into our family home. I remember the lounge having more flowers in it than any florist shop I had ever been in.

I felt lost and empty – it was the weirdest feeling. I was in so much pain and shock that at times I felt numb. It was as if I was looking in on someone else's life. There was so much going on around me that I had no control over. It was a living nightmare. I was overcome with grief, and all I could think was, 'OH, God, Why? Why Gary?' He was the most courageous Christian I have ever known. He had a strong desire to live his life in the service of God. He also loved everyone around him so deeply. I heard him often talk about one day possibly serving the Lord on the mission field, such was his passion for knowing and serving his Lord. I kept questioning why this had happened to him when all he had wanted was to do good. Why couldn't it rather have happened to someone else or a bad person instead?

And All the Days After That...

For the first few days after his passing I was really missing Gary deeply and trying to make sense of it all. But after the funeral was over, the deep dark period of mourning kicked in. Once the business of organising the funeral and the visiting of people had died down, I was left with a huge empty hole in my life. A big dark well of loneliness that was all around me. In times like this you are flooded with various desperate emotions which consume and overwhelm every part of you, leaving you feeling empty beyond what you could ever have imagined. You are left with a constant longing in every fibre of your being just to see your loved one and touch them and talk with them again. You would give anything not to have to live in this new lonely reality. That all-consuming dark pit of despair was everywhere at all times, and there was no way of escaping it.

A few months down the track, my hair started falling out. It didn't all fall out, but there was quite a bit on my pillow each morning. I was told this wasn't uncommon after experiencing a big shock.

I felt totally vulnerable, like only half a person. I felt lost, like I didn't fit in anymore.

When faced with challenges beyond our control, we have a choice: either we can be positive and do our best to get through it, or we can fall into a pit. There were definitely times when I found myself in that pit; but I always climbed back out, albeit in a two-steps-forward, one-step-back kind of way. As we start focusing on moving forward, we begin to see beyond the hurt. If we persist in doing this, then at some point we will start to get our resilience back and be able to feel hope for our future once again.

I think it's great to live in the here-and-now and not think too far ahead. The future can be too overwhelming. Just get through today and tomorrow will take care of itself. But one day you'll start looking forward, one stage at a time. And that's good, because we need to begin to dream again.

> *We have this hope as an anchor for the soul, firm and secure. It enters the inner sanctuary behind the curtain, where our forerunner, Jesus, has entered on our behalf...* (Hebrews 6:19-20)

> *...fixing our eyes on Jesus, the pioneer and perfecter of faith. For the joy set before him he endured the cross, scorning its shame, and sat down at the right hand of the throne of God.* (Hebrews 12:2)

Keep your eyes on Jesus, who both began and finished this race we are in. Learn how he did it. Because he never lost sight of where he was headed – that exhilarating finish in and with God – He could put up with everything else along the way.

The Lord never said we could expect to have an easy life; the road always has its ups and downs. But He did promise us that He would stand by us in every season of our lives, especially in our brokenness. Not only will He be there with us, but also, He will give us the strength and hope to get through it. In those times we need to be grateful for our families and friends who support us. They bring more comfort than words can express. And God Himself comforts us with so many blessings, and places just the right people in our lives at the right times. Once again, you can choose either to take everything for granted or to be grateful for it all.

Really early on, just in the first few moments after being told Gary had gone missing and after coming off the phone to my mum, I heard a gentle whisper in my ear. I can still picture it happening. The voice said, 'You are going to be all right; I'm going to look after you.' Even though I heard that voice, at that time I didn't think much about it – I guess because it was so gentle, and because there was so much about to happen. But I have never forgotten it. Those special moments you have with God stay with you forever.

Looking back, I can see how the Lord has looked after me by putting just the right people in my life at the exact time I needed them. I am very blessed to have had that amazing provision by Him.

It would be so much easier if life were all laughs and we never had to experience loneliness, heartbreak or death. However, this imperfect life takes us on a journey that shows us what's important and what's not. Mostly we simply carry on with things, quite happy to just get by; we often lose sight of who we are in the 'rat race' of life. But when things go really wrong we find that the only true, steadfast and unchangeable thing is the Lord. And He is always there to help us, if we will only turn to Him. He wants us to find our feet again, with freshly-opened eyes that see more clearly than they did before. But all this takes time, trust and faith.

The things that hurt us most in life are often the very same things that reshape us and teach us the value of life and what's important. In the days that followed the funeral, the hardest days of my life, I remember feeling extremely drained, anxious and exhausted. I had swirling thoughts and an overwhelming need to talk with Gary just one more time.

There were times when I lay awake at night feeling desperate and lonely beyond words. I felt hurt and let down. I was also desperate to know why in one moment, just when life had been so perfect, it had suddenly changed. Yet as I look back I see that God

In His Time

was in the midst of it all, bringing such great peace that it leaves me with a feeling of wonder.

> *Blessed are those who mourn, for they will be comforted.* (Matthew 5:4)

Choosing to Live with Purpose

How difficult it was at first doing everything without him. I missed him dreadfully. I had been left in a dark space of loss, grief and pain, and now I had to start processing it. The depth of emotion was overwhelming, like nothing I had ever felt before. The shock, the emotions, the numbness and the disbelief were all so raw. My world had changed that day, and I knew I would never be the same again. Reality was hitting me hard in my face. There was no running away from its ugly force.

Not only was I trying to process everything myself, but I was also dealing with other people's shock and disbelief. I couldn't imagine how I would be able to carry on alone without Gary. I felt so lonely, even though there was a house-full of people there with me. It felt like a big mistake, a bad dream, and not my life. It was so very hard. I kept wondering, 'How am I going to do this alone, without Gary here to pull me along and to encourage me?' He had always been so happy and so full of life. He had been a go-getter; he had always known what he wanted. I loved that about him. How on earth was I going to get through this without his help?

I felt very restless, and just kept hoping so desperately he would walk in and it would all have been one big mistake. I longed for that more than I have longed for anything else in my life. I was still trying to get my head around what had happened.

Through the complicated layers of grief, I realised I needed to make a conscious effort to move forward. I was still young. There was very much a part of me that wanted children, and I didn't want to be alone. In moving on, I didn't have to give up Gary completely – after all, he was a big part of me and helped shape me into who I am today.

As time went by, I found that I was living more intentionally. I chose to keep moving, which enabled me to keep growing, to be more intentional and to gain a greater sense of direction in how I wanted to live.

After going through adversity and years of feeling knocked around by life, I now have resilience. I understand that dark times will only last so long, and that afterwards you emerge with new strength and a new attitude to life. You value family, friendships, nature, and the simple act of going for a walk. You see things with fresh eyes. Life's about learning to embrace that journey with all its twists and turns.

Some people seem to be born with a God-given purpose; they just know what they want, and everything appears to fall into place. But, for most of us, I think it's very much about maintaining the unique journey we have chosen to take, and riding that wave. I know our lives are bigger than the 'here and now'. And it's not all just about our physical lives, for we are more than just bodies and minds – we are spiritual beings. We are here for whatever time God has allocated us, we are blessed with our lives and I know that there is more to life than what we see day-to-day. I don't for a moment think that our final ride in the hearse is our last journey. Rather, it is just the beginning of a whole new existence. And not only that. A life like Gary's, lived with so much love, lives on forever in the hearts of those who love and remember him.

Moving On

AFTER YOU START VENTURING OUT into the world again, you will find that you act differently and do things that you wouldn't have done previously. Like me, you may pursue new friendships, perhaps quite different to those you had before, and start living your life quite differently, in an attempt to normalise it. But, as I found, most of this new way of doing things wasn't good for me, and as a consequence was short-lived.

There was a sadness behind my smile in those days. Life went on as normal for others, and they didn't stop to notice. I can remember driving around thinking, 'Why are people not noticing my pain? I have just lost the most important person in the world to me, and everyone is just carrying on like nothing has happened.'

But *my* life had come to a screeching halt. Nothing seemed familiar anymore. Everything had changed, and there was nothing I could do about it. The longing to go home and slip back into my beautiful old life never left me.

Another thing I had to cope with was the many well-meant things said to me, many of them based on ignorance. It seems that those people that know the least about the situation are often those most ready to give their opinion. It was bizarre and very annoying. However, I was blessed to have family and close friends who went through it all with me, and they were my greatest anchor and support.

And at times like these you sure do find out who your real friends are. When after the funeral I only heard from a few of our friends, I found out very quickly that most of our friends were probably more Gary's friends than mine, because I only heard from a few of them more than a couple of times after the funeral. The friends that were there for me, those people are still very much part of my life today and are incredibly special to me. I learnt very quickly that those friends were like precious jewels, and I will never take them for granted. I learnt the importance of hanging out with them and having them around to talk to. It felt good to have different people to chat with, and to hear their take on things. I learnt the importance of saying 'yes' to people who invited me out to do things with them; I also learnt very quickly that if I said 'no' too often then they soon stopped asking.

Going through any really hard time is more difficult than those who haven't been there yet could ever imagine. However, it does produce perseverance and strength.

Remember, hope for the future requires that we trust God with everything, especially the things we don't understand. But at the time, I didn't understand this, and for years I was left feeling 'ripped off'. I definitely was just in survival mode, doing what I could to fill the void.

> *For now we see only a reflection as in a mirror; then we shall see face to face. Now I know in part; then I shall know fully, even as I am fully known.* (1 Corinthians 13:12)

Photos

Memories of Gary.
Top: Tenting at Whitianga with the family, January 1988.
Bottom: Coffee at Mum and Dad's.

In His Time

*A beautiful day full of gorgeous memories,
14 May 1988.*

Photos

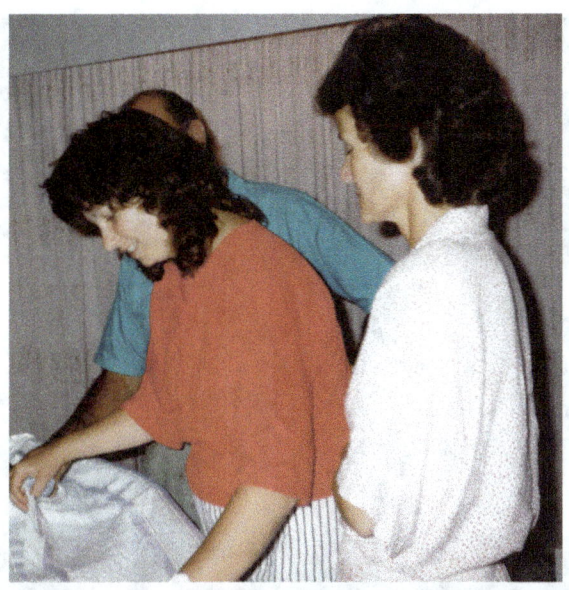

Top: *Spending last precious moments with Gary at the funeral home.*
Bottom: *The day before the funeral, family out at the water hole.*

In His Time

*My amazing family today, January 2022.
I have so much to be grateful for.*

Looking Up

Every so often it is important to remember to look up and to reflect on the wonder of the stars. How majestic and perfect they are, each one placed by God in just the right spot. This always brings home to me the reality of God's perfect plan, and leaves me with feelings of peace, love and wonder. And it gives me strength to go on and face another day.

Each of us has our own unique journey in life, and we can choose to live holding on to the grief of the past or learn to rise above it. If we persist in holding on then eventually it will become too much a part of us and very hard to let go of. This results in bitterness and resentment, which doesn't do anyone any good – least of all ourselves.

In times of grief we can't often see clearly, but years later down the track we are able to look back and see the big picture that we simply couldn't see at the time. But in the early days we can't see past the here-and-now; it's all too hard. The important things we remember, whereas the less important things go by the way. But we always carry the memory of knowing we were loved by that amazing person.

Sometimes you become aware of things that you took for granted before, of spiritual matters that you weren't aware of. You can decide to take them on board or you can ignore them and carry on as normal. Although I was so overwhelmed by everything that had happened, I never stopped thinking about them. There was no denying they were real.

Knowing the without-a-doubt love and comfort of God brought with it a warmth. It was like being held in His arms, wrapped in a secure blanket of pure love and hope. I think that is faith in its purest form. I definitely would never want to go through that time again, that is for sure. But I am grateful for all the amazing blessings sprinkled throughout it. I wouldn't give them up for anything; they are a constant reminder of His love in my life, and I continue to hold on to them.

Life sure is one big wave – sometimes you are riding high, as if there are no cares in the world, and at others you come crashing down and spin out of control. It's a constant ride of ups and downs that can be overwhelming at times.

I see and think more deeply now. I try not to sweat the small stuff, and I'm far more grateful for a lot of what other people simply take for granted. Most of all, I'm grateful that God never pressures us; rather He speaks so that we can hear Him and feel His nearness. But at the end of the day the choice is ours. We can choose to follow Him and have a close relationship with Him, or we can choose to go our own way. The Lord will never pressure us – He is very gracious, and patient beyond words. Believe me, I know; I have tested Him many times in my life, I'm sure. I suppose that people who don't know the Lord don't recognise Him, his voice and see His provision for them. I'm just so thankful that I knew Him and heard Him throughout that time. It was hard enough going through it *with* Him; without Him I really don't know where I would be today.

There have been days when I felt I was going crazy, and there have been others when I could be very thankful for my life. Through it all I have experienced something that has given me a special relationship with God my Maker. It has made me very aware of His grace and love for me.

Memories

GARY WAS EXTREMELY LOVING; he looked at me as if no one else existed. Everyone around us noticed it and talked about it. I remember hearing from Mum that on our wedding day one of her friends noticed how he was looking adoringly at me, like he could 'eat me', as she put it. And that was exactly how he made me feel.

The love we had was amazing; I am so grateful to have had a love like that. Our time together was much like a fairy tale. He was so strong and passionate. We were good together; he brought out the very best in me. We were blessed not to have experienced any major trials and hardships at that stage in our lives, so our time together was not tainted by any form of hardship. We were also very lucky to have been together at a young age – at that stage in life when you simply have fun and don't have to take things too seriously. So I am left with only good memories.

The Funeral Home

Visiting Gary at the funeral home was a very emotional time. It started with the joy of being with him and the excitement of seeing him again, but quickly deteriorated into feelings of 'what the heck'! It wasn't a nice experience, but I want to tell you what happened, because I want this book to be real, honest and informative. People often don't realise the realities that the bereaved have to face behind the scenes. But if you are struggling with your own grief trauma, please look after yourself if you decide to read what follows.

The first visit to the funeral home was okay; he was Gary, my beautiful and very handsome husband. He had his mouth stitched closed, and a patch over one of his eyes as an eel had eaten his eyelid. The second and last visit to see my precious hubby was far more traumatic. As we walked into the room there was a terrible smell, and as I approached him I got the shock of my life. Overnight he had deteriorated so much that he was now pretty much black. I had been given no warning, but I quickly worked out what was happening. I remember being so heartbroken to see his body in that state.

When a person has been in the water for so long (about 19 hours, in his case), their body is saturated with water, and all the microscopic organisms that live in that water have started consuming it, so it starts deteriorating quickly. To this day it still shocks me that they didn't warn us. It was horrible. I sure was experiencing the realities of life and death thick and fast.

In every other way the people at the funeral home were amazing. I guess that even if they had warned me, I still would have gone to see him. At that time all I wanted to do was be near him and to nurture him. Even though I saw Gary like that, I never think about him in that state, or remember him in that way. To me he will always be that larger-than-life character, someone who was loving, gentle and kind.

The Funeral

When it came to planning Gary's funeral, I was very certain of what I wanted. I didn't want anyone to wear all black; we were young, and it was important to not be morbid. Nor did I want a black hearse; I wanted a white or light-silver one. When it came to his coffin, I wanted it to be white. The people at the funeral home made it up specially for him and it was very beautiful, in fact just perfect. I put all my effort into planning his funeral; I wanted everything as perfect as it could be. I put so much love into it, and it was consequently really beautiful. The importance of getting it just right for him became my focus – every song he loved, the perfect casket, and every other detail taken care of. I felt like it was the last thing I could do for him.

For a few weeks after the funeral I felt massively drained, and struggled to comprehend a life without Gary. Reality was never far away. It just took Mum to invite all the family over for dinner, and I usually left the table in tears. Both Gary and I had always loved our family get-togethers; but now, all of a sudden, I was there without Gary next to me. I found this so hard, and it always felt unfair.

I had times when I felt plain angry; angry that this was now my life, angry that Gary had gone swimming, angry that he hadn't come home, and angry with God. Everything seemed so unfair. All of our friends were newly married and starting to have kids; their lives were all on track and happily moving forward. I felt very detached from them all, and I suddenly had nothing in common with them anymore. They were all getting on with their lives, whilst I was in a living nightmare. With every passing week I felt more isolated and lonely. I was happy for the people around me, that they were able to just get on with their lives. But it felt like I had lost everything – Gary, our friends and everything that came along with the happy expectation of being newly married.

My life now felt dark and hopeless. I felt so alone – everyone else had someone close whom they could talk to. I was going through the unthinkable, without Gary to talk to about it. I felt like I was caught in a large wave that was tumbling me around violently and relentlessly. I was constantly tired and felt beaten up by all the emotions in my heart.

When we are grieving deeply in the depths of our souls, this affects our bodies too. In my case, the chest pain was so bad that I felt like my guts had been ripped out. The very rawness of the realisation of the loss, and that things were never going to be the same, made my heart sick.

Be gracious and compassionate to me, O Lord, for I am in trouble; My eye is clouded and weakened by grief, my soul and my body also. (Psalm 31:9, AMP)

The Aftermath

I'M NOT SURE IF TIME HEALS; I think that's just a cliché. It does help soften the pain. But you are still left with a wound that never leaves. Life goes on, but it's very different to what it was before.

When you have gone through something traumatic, it often has long-term effects. For example, to guard against any sort of accident, I never allowed anyone else to look after my children – except for rare occasions when I left them with my sisters or the children's grandparents (and my youngest daughter Eden went into daycare while I completed a diploma). I have always been super-protective of my children, and tended to over-analyse everything. I never wanted to live with any regrets if I could possibly help it. They were and still are the most precious things in my life. So I protected them like their very lives depended on it. I worry about many things and feel like I'm in high-alert mode a lot of the time. And often this is very exhausting. I think these reactions are a consequence of the trauma I went through at such a young age.

The mourning process is a lonely one. Even to this day, over thirty years later, it still sometimes affects me; there are days when I am tearful and need to reset and focus on the here-and-now. I have to remind myself that Gary is happy and in the Lord's hands, and then give it over to God and lean on Him.

I believe that, in God's hands, my greatest pain can become my greatest blessing. I want this book to reach many people and make a difference in their lives. Gary wanted to make a difference in people's lives, so maybe his dying was the way it was going to happen. We understand our lives with limited insight, but *God* sees the big picture. With God's help, I want to walk beside others through their struggles. As I have been writing and thinking back over things, I have come to realise that those old emotions are still there, and that gives me understanding of and empathy for others going through grief.

> *I can do all things through Him who gives me strength.* (Philippians 4:13)

It's so great to be able to draw strength from God, for He *is* our strength. With Christ's strength in my heart, I am able to move forward in the right direction. I simply need to keep fixing my eyes on Him.

Life is incredibly fragile – it can change so fast, and we never know just what tomorrow will bring. When hard things happen, we learn first-hand how difficult life can get, how truly short it is and how bad things can happen to good people.

Marriage

As a little girl, all I ever wanted in my life was to be a wife and a mother. I started adding items to my 'glory box' as soon as I started working, in preparation for when I got married. It was important for me to collect all the things I would need in setting up a home. I had all the towels, sheets, blankets and kitchenware we would need. It was important to me to have a very homely and welcoming home straight away. I am so pleased to say that, as a consequence, Gary and I had everything we needed from Day One.

We lived in a little Lockwood home on the farm where we worked; we were incredibly lucky to have a beautiful home all set up straight away. And I was very much looking forward to spending the rest of my life making a home for Gary.

Marriage is as profound as it is symbolic. When you marry someone, you are joined not just physically but spiritually. Gary's eyes always held so much love for me. God had given us each other on our wedding day.

That is why a man leaves his father and mother and is united to his wife, and they become one flesh. (Genesis 2:24)

That is why after his death I felt such a ripping apart, because the Bible says a couple is joined 'till death do you part'. I was feeling the physical pain of separation. Looking back, I now understand why the Lord wrote these things in the Bible, for they are so true to life. When we experience this we shouldn't be surprised; it's a validation of what He has written in the Bible. It's funny how you can live it and *know* it, but still it can take years to understand it; because it is so big, you need time to fully process it.

I love looking at the special photo album I have, which I put together after Gary died; it contains a lot of our photos and special memories. I love looking through that album and being transported back to each place and each event, every page revealing one memory at a time.

Today I am very happily married to Vaughan. This incredibly precious man allowed me to have another man in my life whilst I was writing this book. When putting pen to paper, I had to go back to that time of grieving and relive my life with Gary, both before and after his death. It has been an incredibly difficult journey, and through it all, Vaughan has been my greatest support. I am sure that not many husbands would be so patient and selfless. I have four adult children and four very precious grandchildren; and I am looking forward to more grandchildren arriving in the future, God willing.

The Supernatural

IT HAS BEEN OVER 32 YEARS since the accident took place. I can still remember everything that happened over that time; it is etched into my mind. But the strongest memories I have are of those things I experienced with the Lord, the spiritual things I can't fully explain, but that no one can take away from me.

About four months after the funeral, my sister Leanne and I were sitting in church, shoulder to shoulder. Suddenly I turned to her and said, 'Gary is here!' I couldn't see him; I could just feel his presence. She was already looking at me with tear-filled eyes, and she replied, 'I know, I can feel him.' Then, as quickly as the feeling came, it was gone again, and I was left wondering if I had just kept quiet and said nothing then it might have lasted longer.

For those few beautiful seconds we both felt his presence again. It was amazing! I would have thought it was in my imagination or my mind playing tricks on me if in that same instant Leanne hadn't experienced it too. It was the last thing I could have ever imagined would happen, even in my wildest dreams. To this day when we talk about it, the hair stands up on Leanne's arms, and the memory brings us both great peace and feelings of wonder.

Back then, I didn't yet have a proper understanding of those kinds of experiences; they were all very new to me and my family. Now I have the knowledge that God is God and He can do anything He chooses. He knows everything, every thought and situation, and sometimes He gives us special moments like these so that we will know that each and every situation is seen by Him and that He is working for our good through it all.

He blesses us with special moments, all uniquely suited to each of us. The Lord sees the big picture and, when we need it, He gives us experiences that bring us reassurance and comfort. He gives us something good that holds meaning in our life from that moment on.

Beautiful moments like that are just so incredible; there are no words to describe them. Those couple of seconds were worth more than any gift anyone could have bought for me here on earth.

Many people get a special glimpse into the supernatural. For some people this comes in instances such as catching an unexpected glimpse of something they can relate to with their loved one like a favourite song on the way to the funeral, noticing the sun shining extra brightly on one favourite flower on the casket, or sensing their presence. Most people who lose someone very close or special to them have a uniquely special story to tell.

I'm not sure why sometimes those of us who have lost someone close to us experience such beautiful moments. Perhaps they are the Lord's way of blessing us and saying, 'Hey, there is a spiritual side to you that you can choose to explore. Here is a glimpse of it.' Whether you are a Christian or not, when you experience these things you can either open your heart and embrace them, or you can ignore them and simply carry on as before. But however you choose to respond, I am sure you will never forget them. The Lord reminds us in the Bible that there is no need to know and understand everything. We simply need to trust Him.

> *Trust in the Lord with all your heart; do not depend on your own understanding. Seek his will in all you do, and he will show you which path to take.* (Proverbs 3:5, NLT)

A few times over the next couple of years, people would mention that they thought it would be a good idea for me to visit a psychic or medium. But I always knew I wouldn't do so because I had grown up knowing what the Bible had to say about that type of thing.

I longed for one more conversation with Gary. But I always knew that if I went to a medium it would be the devil at play, just trying to plant deception in my head. I thought about it long and hard, and always came up with this same answer. I just didn't want to give the devil that opening in my life. Nothing to do with visiting a psychic is consistent with any of God's thinking. He has commanded us not to do so.

Do not turn to mediums or necromancers; do not seek them out, and so make yourselves unclean by them: I am the LORD your God. (Leviticus 19:31, ESV)

For since the creation of the world God's invisible qualities – his eternal power and divine nature – have been clearly seen, being understood from what has been made, so that people are without excuse. (Romans 1:20)

If we want knowledge beyond what our senses can tell us, and we most certainly do, we are to seek that information from God, and from Him alone. The Holy Spirit speaks to us through the Bible, the written revelation of God. Clairvoyants, psychics and occult practitioners have no part in this; all they can provide is a cheap and damning counterfeit.

When you enter the land the Lord your God is giving you, do not learn to imitate the detestable ways of the nations there. Let no one be found among you ... practices divination or sorcery,

> *interprets omens, engages in witchcraft, or casts spells, or who is a medium or spiritist or who consults the dead. Anyone who does these things is detestable to the Lord... You must be blameless before the Lord your God. The nations you will dispossess listen to those who practice sorcery or divination. But as for you, the Lord your God has not permitted you to do so.* (Deuteronomy 18:9-14)

The Bible calls all of these things 'an abomination', so it is very clear we are to keep right away from them.

I am waiting for that beautiful conversation I will have with Gary in Heaven one day. I am very much looking forward to those conversations, for we will be forever together again. Most people in this world want everything right here and now. They want everything at their fingertips. But that's often not God's way. He tells us to be patient and obedient, and to wait for his reward. He promises to supply all our needs here on earth if we love and obey Him, and also promises eternal joy and wholeness in Heaven. Why we have to wait for some answers doesn't make sense to us, but we know we can trust Him. We need to ask Him to *teach* us how to trust Him, for He has promised that he will never leave us nor forsake us.

The Father's Heart

IN WRITING THIS BOOK I have realised how incredibly close the Lord is and has been throughout my journey. He has shown me that even when I thought nobody knew what I was going through, He was a witness to every tear I shed.

We need to create a habit of prayer, of seeking God. And for this we need the Holy Spirit to inspire us. We need to learn to trust in Him despite what is happening in our lives. Even when we feel lonely and He seems distant, we need to remember that he is closer than we could ever imagine.

This world is lost because people can't comprehend the heart and love Jesus Christ has for them. As Christians we are told to weep with the broken-hearted and to love and care for those in need. We have to show compassion, empathy and true love for others in their pain. It's okay if we don't know what to say; it's far more important just to be there for them and to show love and empathy through our actions.

In times of mourning, people need to know that their grief will not last forever, that this season of their lives will give way to happier times. They need to know that we will stand by them and support them, not just until the funeral is over but for as long as they need it.

Time with the Lord

IN THE PAST I LIKED TO REBEL; I thought it made me happy. How wrong I was. But, praise God, this way of life eventually began to feel completely empty and boring, and I started to develop a hunger and thirst for God again. Over time He convinced me of His love. And He filled my life afresh with His Holy Spirit.

God wants a relationship with us; He wants us to know Him, love Him and trust Him. He alone is our hope and refuge. When people let us down, He is always there. He said He wouldn't let us go through any hardships or trials alone. That is why the Holy Spirit was there to carry me, to comfort and support me and to give me those special blessings. The Lord helps us throughout the different seasons of our lives. The Holy Spirit impressed on me the importance of living for God each day, of being 'all in' for Him. Now I can't imagine living life without Him.

Some of us need a wake-up call in our lives so that we can be aware of the presence of the Lord. He is with us on our mountaintop experiences as well as in the dark valleys. We need to engage with Him in every season of our lives. When things get hard and we have questions, then reading the Bible and praying to Him will always bring answers.

The shock of losing Gary was not a surprise to God, for He knew the bigger picture. He was there all the time and never left me. I felt Him there first-hand. Sometimes it takes a trial in life to open our eyes to the realisation that we need to engage with the Lord.

In His Time

For a long time the devil kept me feeling anxious and angry, and in doing so I took my eyes off Jesus. I became too busy for the Lord and too busy for church. But He was very patient with me, even though it took many years for me to realise that I couldn't live my life apart from Him. I slowly began to understand that I needed to focus on Him and be thankful for His many blessings in my life. My circumstances had changed, but God hadn't. He is a God who speaks to our hearts.

A few moments after Gary went missing, the Lord spoke to me. He told me he would never leave me. And He never did. But over time the demands of living and finding my way again made me less aware of Him. But each time I came back to Him, He was there waiting for me. The more I grew to trust Him, the more I began to feel blessed and thankful. Eventually my life quietened and I found peace as I focused on Him.

I am so thankful that I grew up in a Christian home. I am thankful that as a little girl I asked the Lord into my life. I am thankful for the awakening call of the Lord Jesus Christ, and the nudging of his Holy Spirit in my heart.

There is a journey of healing, and it starts with learning to forgive and letting go of anger. It is a massive journey. It began for me when I started saying, 'God, I want you more than I want my old life back again; I don't need to have answers anymore. I feel happy with You.' And then a feeling of contentment came over me, one that I hadn't had since before Gary died. I now have a peace I haven't had for a long time. I know I still have some rough edges, but God can fix them. I remain a work in progress.

I know I need a relationship with Him every day. I need a connection with Him at all times. Jesus loves me just as I am; but the more I surrender to Him, the more He is able to change me into the person He wants me to be. All the while He is there for me, going through everything with me. He forgives my sin and covers me with His love. He created us to live in His love, and to live a life of love – to love Him and our neighbours as ourselves.

We all need a life-changing encounter with the Lord. I often pray, 'Dear Lord, give me the courage to keep surrendering to You, to keep walking with You, and to keep choosing You and your Presence.' We all need God to lead us. And what do we do when He leads us into a place we weren't expecting to go to? We simply trust that it is part of His wise and loving plan for us.

So do not throw away your confidence; it will be richly rewarded.
(Hebrews 10:35)

Walking Through the Valley

AFTER LOSING SOMEONE WE LOVE, we need time to mourn; we need time to let go of them and time to learn to live without them, time to readjust our thoughts. But it is important not to stay there, nor to wallow in self-pity. We need to be determined to come out of it stronger and more focused than we were before. We need it to bring the best out in us. We need to be careful not to let bitterness harden our hearts – the devil will use that to fill our minds with all sorts of deceit. He will use whatever it takes to bring us down and cause more chaos in our lives.

> *The Lord is my shepherd; I have all that I need. He lets me rest in green meadows; He leads me beside peaceful streams. He renews my strength. He guides me along right paths, bringing honour to His name. Even when I walk through the darkest valley; I will not be afraid, for You are close beside me. Your rod and your staff protect and comfort me.* (Psalm 23:1-4, NLT)

As David says in this psalm, we walk *through* the darkest valley but don't have to stay there; we are to keep on moving. God doesn't want us to stay in those low places. Listen for His voice. He will comfort you and walk with you. He will lead you through this valley. We are not to stay there, for that's where depression, fear and worry take over, and where we start questioning Him. Worship God and your mood will shift. He is greater than our questions. Say, 'God, I trust You even though I don't understand

You at times. My love for you is greater than my unanswered questions.' These moments are the best time to start praising Him. When we give praise and sing to Him we feel better, and this quietens whatever else that is going on in our lives. When we put aside the sadness that we're feeling and put on the garment of praise, we can truly say, 'God, you are greater than my understanding of what I am going through; I trust your wisdom, and I will continually hand everything over to you. My hope and trust are in You, my Comforter.'

We need to praise Him even if we don't feel like it. Some of us find it hard to hand everything over to God, but when we do so, the comfort we receive is amazing. Because our focus is on God more than on ourselves, we can begin the healing process. It took time for me to allow myself to make that choice to trust God regardless of my circumstances; but once I had I found that the best thing about handing my problems over to Him was that I no longer had to deal with them on my own anymore. As Gary had always said, He is there 24/7 and he is greater than our circumstances.

Insensitivity

I FOUND IT DIFFICULT WHEN PEOPLE said thoughtless things or asked personal questions. I know they weren't doing so intentionally, but it nevertheless just added to the pain I was dealing with. As lovely as these people were, they sometimes did and said things that caused me even more pain. As a result, I found myself withdrawing. Sometimes it just felt easier not to deal with people who had *no idea* of what I was going through. Which at times felt like everyone on the planet. Just in the first few weeks after the funeral, I was told to 'just get over him', to 'just let him go'; another was 'you're young, you will get over it' and 'you're young, you will find someone else'.

It very quickly became clear to me that most people had no real understanding of my situation at all. So, because I already had so much to cope with and could handle no more, I put up walls of self-protection. I think people forget very quickly that you have just lost your entire world, and that it's going to require a lot of time and effort to restore your life to some form of normality. I had lost my everything that day – my best friend, husband, home, income and almost every bit of security I had.

Much to the contrary of what most people believe, when you are going through a time of bereavement, you *want* to talk about the loved one you have lost. Most people don't understand this, so they are very careful *not* to mention anything to do with them or what happened. They walk on eggshells around you. But most of us absolutely love to talk about them. We are just bursting inside

In His Time

to acknowledge them; it makes us feel close to them. At a time like this there is nothing better than talking about all your treasured memories.

Random Thoughts

THROUGHOUT IT ALL I kept on smiling, though this smile was laced with sorrow; I never wanted to reveal just how raw my emotions were. I found very quickly that as long as you have a smile on your face, the people around you will often be too busy or at times a little shallow to see past it. They will automatically think that all is well, and that you are moving on or getting over it all.

I think people are quick to want to think this because it takes the pressure off them in some way. If you are good at clothing yourself with outward strength, it appears that you are getting on with life, and this makes it easier for them. I didn't want to be the big 'downer' that people would take pity on.

In many ways, to the outside world, it appeared that I was moving on. But inwardly I felt I was losing myself in the process. At times I was left feeling emotionally drained. I was exhausted from the battle inside me as a result of the loneliness and emptiness of having to do life without Gary. It was as if someone had pulled my guts right out, and I couldn't have felt more vulnerable and empty. My entire existence was centred around surviving from day to day.

I cried out to God, 'Lord, I have so many questions. There are so many unknowns about my tomorrows. In the Bible your Word tells me you have great plans for me – why couldn't it have been great plans for both Gary and me together?' I had so many unanswered questions rolling around in my head.

Coping with Grief

IT IS IMPORTANT TO HAVE a good old cry at times, and for that matter a good laugh as well. They both are healing and quite normal. Back in the past, when someone died, their photos were often taken down off the walls and they were never spoken about again. The families preferred to 'push things under the carpet'; I guess that was their coping mechanism. I always struggled with that mentality. I never for a moment wanted that sort of thinking in my life. I always wanted to celebrate Gary's life and keep his memory alive. I liked to talk about Gary because he was never far from my mind; the more I could talk about him, the happier I felt. He had lived, and his life was worth celebrating.

Our friends were also all dealing with the loss of Gary and grieving in their own way. Because none of them had ever gone through anything like this before, they all handled it differently. They had no understanding of what I was going through; they couldn't possibly have known. My grief was so acute that there was no way of understanding it unless they had experienced it for themselves. Consequently it was a difficult time for everyone. Thankfully I did have friends and family that kept showing up and inviting me out. Those special people were the ones who kept me going.

Not too many people escape some sort of hardship in their lives. Most people are able to understand and help others who have experienced the same type of pain that they have been through. It's important to find the right people to help you.

There was one special girl in my church at the time. Although she was married and had three kids, she was always there for me. She would ring me and take me roller skating, something that we all enjoyed back then. Or we would just chat. Times out like that made me feel normal, and it was fun. It was a relief to get out of Morrinsville and be a normal fun-loving person again. And hear myself giggle again. Those times spent with her were awesome. I have always felt a lot of gratitude to her for those nights out.

The road l have travelled in my life (and the adversity I have been through) has set me up to become a strong person. I know my own mind, and have become much more resilient than I was before.

Remember, our hope and restoration require that we trust God with everything, especially the things we don't understand.

> *'For my thoughts are not your thoughts, neither are your ways my ways,' declares the Lord. 'As the heavens are higher than the earth, so are my ways higher than your ways and my thoughts than your thoughts.'* (Isaiah 55:8-9)

The loss and grief felt by those around me was nothing compared to the loss I was experiencing, or should I say it was different. I do not believe for one moment that it was less tragic or devastating for both our families, but at the end of the day everyone else had someone to go home to. They all had someone going through it with them, whom they could talk to. *Oh, how I longed so desperately for that.*

It's very hard to explain your own perception of grief because everybody's perception is so different. Losing your partner or a child is so different to losing other relationships, because it affects every single aspect of your entire life.

I was talking to Gary's parents recently about the day of Gary's drowning. His mum told me her side of the story. She had just arrived home from work and had started cooking their dinner when, all of a sudden, she felt extremely ill. It hit her suddenly, so much so that she had to go and lie on the couch. That would have been the exact time Gary died. I have heard of this type of thing happening once before; almost the exact same thing, only in this case it was with brothers. It amazes me how we have such a strong spiritual connection with the people we are closest to. There are more spiritual things happening around us and in us than we realise. We may not be aware of these things in our minds, but our bodies often are affected in some way.

This fascinates me and makes me want to find out more. These types of experiences are just the proof we need that there is more 'out there' than meets the eye. It brings an inexplicable joy, a sense of elation, to be given special moments such as these. Not so much at the time, but later, when you have had time to think about it. They give me hope and confirmation that God is at work.

Often it's not until someone close to us dies that we get to experience this deep spiritual connection. We all have a spirit; the question that each one of us has to ask ourselves is whether we have surrendered it to God or to the things of this world; to Him and His everlasting life or to earthly things that will someday perish.

Other inexplicable things happened to us after Gary's passing; sensing him when we were sitting in church, the peace I had after Gary drowned and all the way through the funeral, and Mum's own experience. These experiences and feelings come seemingly out of nowhere, and they overwhelm you. You can't explain them. They bring such a feeling of peace and reassurance in the midst of shock and devastation. At the time you can't explain them; they require insight in order to appreciate them from an earthly perspective.

Mum was blown away by her experience. She knew seeing Gary in the way she did could only mean one thing – that he was dead.

And consequently she knew to ring the police. But it took her months to actually get her head around it enough to share it with me, because she had never experienced anything like that in her life. Despite even the subsequent adversity of Dad's sudden death three years and two months after Gary's passing, Mum has never again experienced a vision like the one she saw then.

I think that at different times in our lives we are given a greater awareness of things around us. Perhaps a bit like a blind person has enhanced senses of touch and smell. It is at times like this, in the worst of circumstances, that we are sometimes blessed to get a glimpse of the spiritual realm. The warmth of those blessings saturates our soul and give us something lasting to think about. For me, over 30 years on, this still holds true. Some of us perhaps need to go through experiences like these in order to challenge our narrow-minded views and attitudes. They open our eyes to the possibility that God is real and that He cares.

Anxiety

AFTER ALL THIS TIME, I still suffer from some anxiety, although it has settled down compared to what it was. Most days I feel a little anxious, but now I know it's my reminder to keep handing everything over to the Lord; so that's how I deal with it. And as soon as I ask Him to take it away, He does.

Cast all your anxiety on Him because He cares for you. (1 Peter 5:7)

I remember going into town and walking around looking for anyone that had anything in common with Gary – dark hair, same height, anything that I could associate with him. I would see some random person and be amazed that they looked like him from behind. I was searching for anyone that looked familiar, even though I knew he was gone. I just had to keep looking for anything and anyone I could find that would make me feel close to him.

It was so hard to accept it was real, that Gary was gone, and that I couldn't go and visit him. I longed for just one more look at him, just more time to hold him, just one more time to tell him how much I loved him.

Acres of Hope

I'll turn Heartbreak Valley into Acres of Hope. (Hosea 2:15, The Message)

THE HOLY SPIRIT HIGHLIGHTED this verse for me. These days I have acres of hope. And that is what I am choosing to hang on to. I now am starting to see the big picture; I now understand my past more clearly than I ever have before. I can see where the devil got into my head and had a field day with my thinking. Back then lack of self-esteem, too high expectations of other people, my tendency to take things too much to heart, and my inability to bounce back were all problems for me. Now I am feeling stronger, and hopefully greater resilience will come with that. I remain a work in progress. I regularly pray, 'God, grant me the serenity to accept the things I cannot change, the courage to change the things I can, and the wisdom to know the difference.' When you have wrestled over something for so long, you learn to very quickly be thankful. It is not until you *lose* your peace that you really understand its incredible value in your life.

For I can do everything through Christ, who gives me strength. (Philippians 4:13, NLT)

It is my prayer that we will pay more attention to the blessings and miracles that are happening around us; that we will be more aware of all the special things that we experience. We are never going to fully understand the supernatural side of life. The Lord has told us in the Bible that this side of Heaven we will not understand everything. But one day when we get there, we will know everything!

Here are some quotes from Charles Stanley which I've found to be true in my life:

- The dark moments of our life will last only as long as is necessary for God to accomplish His purpose in us.
- Trusting God means looking beyond what we can see to what God sees.
- Brokenness is God's requirement for maximum usefulness.
- Obedience always brings blessing.
- Adversity is a bridge to a deeper relationship with God.
- We learn more in our valley experiences than on our mountain tops.
- God does not require us to understand His will, just obey it – even if it seems unreasonable.

I waited far too long to be obedient to God. In writing this book, I am being obedient. I know without a doubt that the Lord wanted me to tell my story. I love the following verses:

> ...*being confident of this, that he who began a good work in you will carry it on to completion until the day of Christ Jesus.* (Philippians 1:6)

> *Now to him who is able to do immeasurably more than all we ask or imagine, according to his power that is at work within us.* (Ephesians 3:20)

Hope is very much a choice. We have the ability to decide

whether to allow our hope to rise above our despair. God always gives us the choice. That is why He gave us a free will. Otherwise we would be like robots, with no control over any of our decisions, and that would be very boring. We need to activate our hope in Jesus, because what we do today determines our outcomes tomorrow. And what we listen to determines who we become.

> *You belong to your father, the devil, and you want to carry out your father's desires. He was a murderer from the beginning, not holding to the truth, for there is no truth in him. When he lies, he speaks his native language, for he is a liar and the father of lies.* (John 8:44)

> *Wait for the Lord; be strong and take heart and wait for the Lord.* (Psalm 27:14)

> *In all this you greatly rejoice, though now for a little while you may have had to suffer grief in all kinds of trials. These have come so that the proven genuineness of your faith – of greater worth than gold, which perishes even though refined by fire – may result in praise, glory and honour when Jesus Christ is revealed.* (1 Peter 1:6-7)

How vast God is! He has not called us to live in a box or under any restraints. I have found that life with Christ has provided more freedom than I ever experienced without Him.

> *And I ask Him that with both feet planted firmly on love, you'll be able to take in with all followers of Jesus the extravagant dimension of Christ's love. Reach out and experience the breadth, tests its length, plumb the depths, raise to the heights, live full lives, full in the fullness of God.* (Ephesians 3:17-19, The Message)

For a long time after the accident my goal was to make life more bearable, to do what I needed to do to just keep on moving, and to avoid more pain. I simply put one foot in front of the other. But I learnt over time that God wants us to live free and open lives, not merely to constrain ourselves to just getting by. He wants us to focus on Him and receive so much more than we have in the here-and-now. Just getting by week after week doesn't offer us any hope. We have to wake up to the knowledge of the God of the universe. He has so much more to offer us than we can either imagine or deserve. His amazing love can fill us with a peace and a sense of belonging that you won't find anywhere else. We need to 'breathe in' God; we need to let this wealth of knowledge fill our lives. Then we will begin to relax and flourish, knowing that He has our lives in His hands. He sees the big picture, and He is going before us and guiding us toward new beginnings, if we will only put our trust in Him. Then He will give restoration to our soul, and hope for our tomorrows. The future can sometimes seem overwhelming, but if you put it in God's hands you won't have to worry; He will carry your worries and burdens for you.

When I was going through tough times in my life, I often let my emotions rule my thinking and the way I conducted myself. I stayed in a place of anger and frustration for many years, and this affected every area of my life. It takes time to process things, to clarify your thoughts, to reinvent your dreams and to restructure your life.

I am pleased with what the Lord is now doing in my life – the new people He has brought into it are amazing. As we 'breathe' the Lord in, He gets rid of our despair. He restores us and starts changing us, recompensing us for the heartache and emptiness. He gives us the power to overcome our problems. Now I know I will continue to grow through it all, if I allow Him to help me.

How can I learn to be grateful again after losing Gary? By trying not to focus on my loss, and instead to give thanks for the good things I have. In other words, by counting my blessings. I like to think of blessings as God's favour over my life. He shows us favour whether we deserve it or not. We need to be refuelled with the grace of Jesus, the Son of God, who holds us securely.

Disillusioned

Whenever I felt disillusioned, I wanted to rebel. For a time this hardened my heart to the things of God and allowed the devil to gain a foothold in my life. He started filling my mind with thoughts that I would never measure up. And I let my broken heart turn into a disillusioned one, and this fed my insecurities. On the outside it didn't show, and most people would never have known what was happening in my head. But for many years this feeling of not being good enough, of not measuring up to other people and their expectations, ate me up. Even to this day I struggle with this in some measure, and need to keep reminding myself to keep handing it over to Jesus. I try to be around people who are loving and kind. By focusing on Jesus, I have learnt not to overcomplicate things.

With my disillusionment came discouragement, depression, anxiety, fear and dread. I was a hypocrite, not living what I knew to be right in my heart. I lived to please others, because in doing so I felt more accepted. I ended up doing things to please people, all the while knowing in my heart this was not pleasing to God. But this only left me feeling compromised and empty most of the time. Because I knew that I desperately needed to change, I eventually made a decision to surrender my life to God. I have learnt that it's not about what others think of me, but about where I am with the Lord. I know that He, not the person standing next to me, gives me the validation I need.

Our Lord wants us to have a simple devotion to Him, one

which quietens our hearts and gives us an inner strength. We need to do our part by talking to Him in prayer, reading His Word and being obedient to Him. We need to replace worldly expectations with His love. We need to establish a prayer-life. Talking to God changes everything, it puts everything into perspective. This needs to become a daily habit, so that when life becomes shaky and uncertain, we have the firm foundation of Jesus Himself to lean on. Once we have learnt to trust Him, we will then hand all our burdens over to Him. The Bible says we are to cast ALL our burdens on the Lord.

> *Come to me, all you who are weary and burdened, and I will give you rest. Take my yoke upon you and learn from Me, for I am gentle and humble in heart, and you will find rest for your souls.* (Matthew 11:28-29)

> *He gives strength to the weary and increases the power of the weak.* (Isaiah 40:29)

God did not design us to carry our burdens alone. He gives us people around us who can identify with us in our struggles. When you go through things in life, such as a huge tragedy, especially at a young age, it has a huge effect on you; you can so easily be led down wrong paths because you are so vulnerable. For a long time I kept a lot of people at arm's length, I guess because I didn't feel they were ever on the same page as me. Looking back, though, throughout my journey God has surrounded me with people that follow Him.

Church Life

I HAD FAITH FOR SALVATION, but I was 'watery' in putting my faith in God when the hard times came. Instead of standing firm, I let myself get tumbled around, and I was very unsettled for a time. But God was all the while waiting patiently for me to hand over my questions, hurts and anger. Over time I went to a few churches, but always felt like I didn't quite belong. I am thankful now that I kept on trying different ones until I found a good fit.

Finally, I found a church that offered love in a non-judgemental way; one where I could be myself and not feel like I had any expectations hanging over me. It was and is a good fit for me and my family. Today I can walk into that church and feel proud to be a part of it. It's a church that is welcoming to anyone who walks in; there's so much love there that it's a pleasure to be part of it.

If you don't feel a part of your church family, you do need to go 'church-hopping' until you find a good fit for yourself and your family. It is so important to be in fellowship with like-minded people; to find a place where you feel comfortable and where you can relax, get to know others and support one another. Churches are families full of people with different personalities. You need to be part of one where you feel relaxed and happy, and where you want to become more and more involved.

Much like in other areas of life, the more you put into it, the more you get out of it. That is why there are so many different churches, each with its own style; so we can find the right fit

In His Time

for each of us. The one main thing to check on before choosing a church for yourself is that everything taught there is from the Bible and nowhere else.

God's Promises

THE HOLY SPIRIT WILL GIVE you clarity as you speak the Word of God over your life.

As Priscilla Shirer says, 'It requires spiritual discernment, it requires spiritual insight, to be able to see the things that cannot be seen in the physical realm, to be able to hear the things you cannot hear unless the Holy spirit heightens your spiritual ears.'

I have encountered God and His wonderful power many times, and I am trusting Him to help me once again in writing this book. I have learnt that it is the very moment you BELIEVE one of God's promises that it is activated in your life. His greatest promise was that Jesus would die for our sins and be raised to life again on the third day. And that after he was taken back to Heaven, He would send His Holy Spirit to live and work in the hearts of those who believe. Not only did that *actually* happen, but it was the start of many other wonderful promises. Here are some of the things He has promised to those who believe in Him:

- He has promised to love me.
- He has promised to stand by me, and to be with me in my valleys.
- He has promised to bless me.
- He has promised to be there for me and never leave me (and I can testify that this is true).

But blessed is the one who trusts in the Lord, whose confidence is in him. They will be like a tree planted by the water that sends out its roots by the stream. It does not fear when heat comes; its leaves are always green. It has no worries in a year of drought and never fails to bear fruit. (Jeremiah 17:7-8)

This is the confidence we have in approaching God: that if we ask anything according to his will, he hears us. And if we know that he hears us – whatever we ask – we know that we have what we asked of him. (1 John 5:14)

From Despair to Faith

THINGS CAN GET QUITE DARK AT TIMES – grief and loss are not an easy thing. God understands that. But we can begin to make the journey from despair to faith.

Despair = to be in a place with no hope.
Hope = the simple belief that things *will* change.
Faith = the reality of things hoped for.

God says that all things are possible to those who believe. *All* things. Believe in His promises. Wait on Him. He will make a way in your life so that His will may be done in and through it. Draw near to Him and He will draw near to you (James 4:8). It is a privilege to be in God's presence.

Life is tough at times, but it's in those times that new people come into our lives; those we never expected it from reach out to us in ways that are such a blessing. As this happens, new relationships are formed. Also, old friendships take on a new appreciation, and a greater love for people in general starts developing.

The greatest comfort I have had in all of this was that I knew without a doubt Gary was in Heaven with the Lord. What a fantastic thing to know. I never once wondered if I would ever see him again. I know where he is. I was never prepared to give him up, to relinquish the dreams we shared. It took a long time to get my head around that.

There is beauty in the name of Jesus, and that was my turning point. While we are on this earth, things are not ever going to be perfect. We are living in a fallen world, where the devil is at play. But God opens our eyes to the truth of who Jesus is, and we then become aware of the reality of these two vastly different worlds. And we can choose to live in the kingdom of this world or in the Kingdom of God.

The sorrows of living in an imperfect world will eventually bring us to our knees. Then we will be so blessed to know that, if we keep our eyes on Jesus, there is a perfect place called Heaven waiting for us. The Bible gives us many beautiful promises of what we can expect there – no more grief, no more sorrow, no more tears and no more separation. All these negative things belong to the time we have here on this earth. We all at some stage have to come face to face with the realities of living in a sinful world.

I choose to keep my eyes on the Lord Jesus. He alone gives me strength; He alone is who I choose to put my faith in. I am so thankful that He is all around me, comforting me in special ways. We just have to live with open eyes and an open heart to Him. We need to learn to know God, to know His voice and to know His beautifully unique ways. And to recognise that He is in the big picture of our lives. God knows the reality of death, having experienced the grief of the death of his only Son, Jesus. He knows first-hand that pain we bear in our loss. It is no surprise to Him, which is why I think He floods us with beautiful blessings that keep us going.

Hope is here; it's a free gift. It gives us a peace that surpasses all understanding. You just have to remember that the Lord is with you in every circumstance of your life. You just have to talk to Him and acknowledge Him, and He will talk back to you. Ask Him to show you how much He loves you and learn how to wait on Him to give you all you need.

It's mind-blowing that God is with us; that His presence, His

Holy Spirit, will come and make His home in us, if we will only obey Him (see John chapter 14). He's there on our mountain tops and in our valleys. It's mind-blowing to be a son or daughter of the Living God. It's hard to comprehend that a God so vast and all-powerful would even bother with us, let alone be so tender towards us.

> *...how often I have longed to gather your children together, as a hen gathers her chicks under her wings, and you were not willing...* (Matthew 23:37)

At times I feel so unworthy of His love. We just need faith the size of a tiny mustard seed (that's all that God requires) in order to believe in Him and His promises. And if we don't have even that tiny amount of faith to believe in Him, we can ask Him to give it to us, *and He will*! That is His amazing promise to us.

A Relationship with God

IT IS A PRIVILEGE TO HEAR God's voice. Jesus calls us all into relationship with Him. This is more than just knowing about Him, it's about putting our trust in Him. He calls Himself the Good Shepherd and us the sheep. He says that His sheep hear His voice (John chapter 10). When you're discouraged and overwhelmed, you need to seek God. Jesus says that all power in Heaven and on earth has been given to Him (Matthew 28:18), so it makes no sense seeking anyone or anything other than Him. He holds all the power.

The problem with us is that we are never satisfied, and we always want more. But we don't go to God with our questions and needs. We rather look for answers in all the wrong places. Then we have the devil saying in our ear, 'It won't hurt; just do it.'

In fact, all we need to do is to open up our Bible and seek God. He truly loves us and will therefore provide us with the *right* knowledge. The Bible says that we have to seek first the Kingdom of God. In doing so we will find our purpose in Him, and He will fill that longing in our hearts for a life of true purpose and joy. We have to remember we do not need to question God's ways. We can trust in His power, wisdom and love, and in His ability and desire to make all things well.

I haven't got all the answers; I just know what I have experienced. And each and every one of those moments have been an incredible blessing to me.

In Closing

THE LORD IS THERE for every falling tear. Writing this book has been very confronting for me. God asked me to do it, so I told Him that He needed to give me the words. After going through all the tough times, He has given me an opportunity to impact the lives of others through my writing, and it is an amazing gift.

Each and every time I sat down to write, which was quite often at two o'clock in the morning, I would first pray. I would ask God to tell me what He wanted me to talk about, and instantly I would feel as if I was right back in that time and place, the emotions just as fresh. Then I would simply start writing what came to mind.

It was surprising to me to find how those feelings so easily bubbled up to the surface again. It's been a long time since Gary's death, and I thought a lot of the raw emotion had gone. But I was wrong. They were the most difficult things to write about, and the very things I asked God to remind me of; and when I did, they were instantly there again. Before I prayed there were memories, but the rawness, the sting, no longer had a hold on me. So my first thought was, 'How am I going to write how I actually felt at that time; how will I convey the raw, dark pain I felt back then?' That is why I had to lean on God and trust Him to take me back to those darkest times.

It was amazing to feel God's presence so strongly during the writing of this book; to ask for His help, and instantly be placed back 32 years in time. It made me realise that the Lord had been with me in every moment of my grief. I had known He was, but now He was showing me at a far deeper level. I am so grateful for this experience, for it has taught me so much about the God I love; how He is there listening to every conversation and thought, and answering every prayer. How He has been there all the time.

In being obedient to God I have come to realise just how incredibly close He is, for in writing this book I have been reminded of things I had no idea anyone else knew. I had kept a lot to myself, or so I thought. But God showed me He had always been there, even in the darkest of dark days, and that not one tear had gone unnoticed.

If I had not stepped out in faith and written this book, I never would have realised how close the Lord really was. There is a new hope flowing through my veins now, one that has no doubt that the Lord knows everything and that He has got us under his protective wing. I am in awe of this God I trust and adore. I'm still not sure why the Lord wanted my story in print, but I am confident that He has a plan for it. And in writing it I have gained so much that it's mind-blowing. It has given me a much deeper appreciation for the wonderful husband I am so blessed to now have – I am rich beyond words. The Lord saw every one of my tears. We live our lives by faith, not sight, as we walk into a future that only God knows. In the words of the lovely Maranatha Music song by Linda Ball that we used to sing in church growing up, and which came to my mind often in the days following Gary's death:

In His time, in His time,
He makes all things beautiful, in His time;
Lord, please show me every day,
as you're teaching me your way,
that you do just what you say,
in your time.

This song was played in instrumental form as Gary's coffin was carried from the church during his funeral.

The Beginning?

EVEN BEFORE I KNEW Gary was dead, just after I was told he was missing, I felt my mind and body being gently led, taken over by a peaceful feeling. Immediately I sensed the Lord's comforting presence and heard His voice whisper in my ear, 'You are going to be all right; I will be with you always; I will look after you.'

Even today, that memory is so real. It was a profound moment when God simply let me know that He was there for me. That feeling of being surrounded by God's presence was all-consuming. Thinking back on it now, it was amazing; and I feel extremely grateful.

In the next few years after Gary's death our family went through the loss of six more family members in close succession. My father, three uncles and my two grandmothers. We got to wondering if it was ever going to stop. For Mum, it was like a hurricane going through her life.

Although Gary's body died that day, he has never been more alive than he is now, with His Lord. Gary simply went home to be with Him that day.

The Lord gives us the victory to overcome the sting of death.

I have faith in God who is fully able to do all the things He has promised in His Word. I feel that this terrible experience has given me a depth and strength I never had before, even though I have never considered myself to be a strong person.

Having the photos of the funeral as a reminder, especially the two of me spending my last moments next to Gary in his coffin at the funeral home, I feel I have something tangible that I can look at when I have needed to. They are a great reminder that it happened. When you go through something as big as this, your mind plays tricks on you, and sometimes it doesn't feel real; it can all just feel like a bad dream, or someone else's life. I don't know who took the photos, but I have been extremely grateful for them over the years.

Therefore, do not worry about tomorrow, for tomorrow will worry about itself. Each day has enough troubles of its own. (Matthew 6:34)

The Holy Spirit speaks to us in many different ways. Occasionally when he talks to you, you can actually hear His voice; it's as clear as if He were sitting beside you in the next chair, or like a spoken thought you didn't think. I have experienced this three times so far in my life. But it doesn't matter whether you hear His voice out loud or whether He impresses you deeply in your spirit – both ways you *know* it is Him. We need to activate our faith in the Lord. We need to hand every situation over to Him.

For the word of God is alive and active. Sharper than any double-edged sword, it penetrates even to dividing soul and spirit, joints and marrow; it judges the thoughts and attitudes of the heart. (Hebrews 4:12)

Even though the Bible was written thousands of years ago it is still completely relevant for us today. Therefore the Bible is referred to as the living Word, because it's alive and active and works in us to change us. I have placed Bible verses throughout this book in order to show the relevance they provide for us today.

God never promised it would be easy, but He did promise we

would never be alone. The importance of knowing where we are going to be spending eternity cannot be over-emphasised. Eternity lasts for ever; we are going to spend a long time there. So we need to know where we are choosing to go. People need to put in more thought about this as they go about their lives.

I had no idea when I woke up that morning that the Lord would ask me to start writing a book that day. That last day I had with Gary, the day he drowned, we had no idea that at about 6.15 pm he would be in Heaven. For many people, their eternity is much closer than they would ever like to imagine. When you go through adversity like I did, it brings home very swiftly the cruel reality of that fact. None of us has any idea what the next few moments in our lives will bring.

We are so used to thinking we are in control, and it's very easy to just keep busy and not give it a moment's thought. The fact is none of us knows what the next moments will bring. Most people do not get a lingering disease that allows them time to think about such things. So you need to be ready for life and whatever it throws at you. You do not want to die with regrets. We never get to choose which valleys we have to walk through, but God is always there with us, going before us...

The Lord is calling us to a life of strength, peace and purpose. We can only gain this through Him. If we hand our life over to Him in obedience and love, He will fill it to overflowing with His love, joy and peace.

www.ingramcontent.com/pod-product-compliance
Lightning Source LLC
Chambersburg PA
CBHW051453290426
44109CB00016B/1740